IN THE CITY OF

SMOKING MIRRORS

Camino del Sol

A Latina and Latino Literary Series

Albino Carrillo

IN THE CITY OF

SMOKING MIRRORS

The University of Arizona Press   Tucson

The University of Arizona Press
© 2004 Albino Carrillo
First Printing
All rights reserved

♾ This book is printed on acid-free, archival-quality paper.
Manufactured in the United States of America

09 08 07 06 05 04 6 5 4 3 2 1

Library of Congress Cataloging-in-Publication Data

Carrillo, Albino, 1964–
In the city of smoking mirrors / Albino Carrillo.
p. cm. — (Camino del sol)
ISBN 0-8165-2325-8 (alk. paper)
1. Aztec gods—Poetry. 2. Reincarnation—Poetry. 3. Prophecies—
Poetry. I. Title. II. Series.
PS3603.A7745 I5 2003
811'.6—dc21

2003010301

British Library Cataloguing-in-Publication Data
A catalogue record for this book is available from the British Library.

Publication of this book is made possible in part by the proceeds of a
permanent endowment created with the assistance of a Challenge
Grant from the National Endowment for the Humanities, a federal
agency.

Dedications

Prelude: War Kept Huitzilopochtli from Dreaming of Travel
for Caryn Connelly

Una Raza de Gigantes
for Juli Kroll

"De las Diez Estrellas . . ."
for Jefferson Adams

H. Writes to His Brother . . .
for Rudy Carrillo

Discovering a Christian Hymnal
for Norman Dubie

H. Writes to Bear . . .

for Henry Quintero

Contents

I would like to extend deep appreciation and thanks to Caryn Connelly and Juli Kroll for the love and support they offered during the writing of the manuscript. Also, thanks to Karyn Huggett for helping format the manuscript. Thanks to the Department of English at the University of Minnesota and the Department of English at Union College, New York, without whose facilities this book would not have been written.

This book is for my family.

1.

A tu tierra grulla, que ésta no es tuya.

Prelude: War Kept Huitzilopochtli

from Dreaming of Travel

After a while, the radio became
the only medium in the house: rabid
edicts sent islands of panic quivering
through his sternum, so that his fists grew numb
at night from sleeping near the alarm clock.
They were not songs from cool youth he awoke to
but crack and bursts of static
from the desert of death in the East.

Turning one morning did he recount
to the odd woman who kept his company
how even the slightest bit of talk between
them was better than the stars or the poems
they'd peeled off each other's thighs,
that they'd killed in bed together.

War, daft diction of the media invention
keeps everyone apart! Imagining
how the sun might work H. decided
he was sad, and feared every bit of his
sin boiling away in some Atlantic
missile strike he read about. You see,
science fiction means nothing to the people
in charge of gassing their bombers

about our green planet like they were
just strolling along, in love. Maps of where
we're all hiding are tucked in front pockets,
like cigarettes or condoms—dreaming
this means we'll have no bodies in the
new world gathering in the wary clouds.

But I thought I'd write you anyway
to remind you how H. found himself
at lunch in a hotel restaurant
dwarfed by his latest muse's eyes—all
the plates stopped sliding and soda
glasses vibrated in the trim air when
they spoke and knew each other's faces
beyond the crimson table where they exchanged

some brute knowledge of erotica—
they knew upstairs in suites that couples
were stripping in view of flat objective
hotel mirrors, that drunks were watching CNN
while all along the war flew about them
like a kite lost to clumsy hands or sudden gusts.

Over ten years had passed when H. withdrew
himself to the cool blue basement clutching
the stories that sustained him. What was left
over he took with him up North to live
away from the ocean or mountains,
wherever he might find a small goddess
singing her poems in the midst of quietude
or beer. The prairie grain growing

after winter was never lost to his
dripping Buddha ears. Went H. then
from oracle to oracle expecting
prophesy to double his memory,
stupid, unaware that love tossed about him
like errant paper slipping in the wind.

It was the quick note of one old Mexican
clock which awoke Huitzilopochtli
to find the war mechanized and framed
around famous American sayings
used even when the Gringo General
stood on the Temple of the Sun in 1847.

It's not as though an attack wouldn't do—
everything's off, the fifth world is careening

like the double-barreled human engine
that battered the Pentagon on a still morning
when we were all stuffing our faces in peace,
H. himself running through thickets
of unbelievable late summer sumac,
drowning in his patience, waiting for words.

After a while, he'd walk to the woods
to call his muse on a cell phone—the basement
wouldn't do. He could feel the telegraphic signal
of what he thought was love emanating
from the microwave pulses sustaining
the conversation. It was winter.
The trails he walked were small game trails
where little foxes slept

under thick cottonwood roots. H. wanted
so badly to tell her of the animal rites
he'd observed, but this grim muse
knew nothing of nature: her world
was manners, clean-marbled mansions,
she only waiting to sleep in the suburbs.

One thing he admired was how it all
separated like a loaf of bread if thought
about long enough under cloudy summer
skies—swallows flew in warm drafts & goshawks
watched the green ground from their shrouded
hideouts in trees two miles from where H. kept
his little journal of the war. There was
never any consolation for the series of slightly

filled thought balloons that rose like second guesses
after waking. Whether dream or late-night
movie, what remained that morning harshly

crafted in paper, on a note-card from
a five & dime store left shining in the rain,
was the last letter he'd write to his future tribe:
O, it was so that year. Without disciples
or scribes he'd go mad. This war would take its
trim engines for a tour of his soul—
he'd wake up every morning grinding
his teeth, and as if he'd slept on fists
his thumbs would burn as he wrote this
digested planet news after lovely
talks on the patio with his lover

about summer becoming an impossible space
since its fruition couldn't intimidate
the noon sounds of traffic or frame mundane
prayers each might've made for each other
secretly, when they knew not whence
their passage would start, what it would mean to drift.

Gift

It was the dark black smoke of la grifa
that killed Nevarez one night in April
as he sat in bed, hands on the only
woman who loved him. There wasn't cruel light
from the mirror or the sun, there wasn't
any transcription from another world
etched into the ether either. But love
drifts this way and that, a balloon he saw

near the edge of his life, the lights going now.
It was the dark black smoke of Hiroshima
that burned him into el otro lado
not the woman who loved him but a dream
of a cruel light, a mirror from the sun
floating over every city on earth.

Huitzilopochtli Is Conceived in an Interstate Motel Room

From what city were you writing when
the millennium crystallized downtown
and the proud atom city grew with each
new scientist into the sky? It was
a common dream that brought us under
the Tiffany desk lamp lighting your room—
it was summer and the neighbors behind
this tract home's walls heard you speak

the Roman tongue of my father. In a small room
overlooking the interstate I undressed
you to find the source of your river, O
that you are impossible, your body
unknown. But it began with love, pulling
at your thighs, your hips.

Una Raza de Gigantes

Fué posible. I talked with one last night.
Saw her living in the dark, heard her heart
sway in that corner space around my heart—
but in the holes where we keep our souls
there was something like a monster bearing
down upon our world like a magnet
intergalactically to crush it.
Strike no arrows could this creeping steel

mess that'll touch us all at night sleeping
as we must, away from the world like this,
curled into bodies, dark airplanes overhead
all night and the inevitable loss we create when
waking or touching the visible world,
skin that I love so much and can never let go.

De los Hombres Peores

My father, dreamer from Chihuahua, seemed
alone in his anger. By this he meant
to show us how the world had given up
on him, how the gringos made him bite
his tongue, like an apple over and over
again. This much is true. He never knew
the words to calm his spirit down—angry
was he, reversed, who couldn't speak without

seeming terribly alone. You see
we saw the terrible place from where
this anger grew. A lot in Las Cruces,
a point in the sun, all of the children
hungry and fighting for something better—
the green stars, the fluorescent border highways.

De las Mujeres Tristes

My mother, beauty queen from Rincon, seemed
alone in her sadness. By this she meant
to show us how the world had given up
on her, how the angels made her bite
her lips like plums over and over
again. This much was true. She never knew
the words to fill her body with love, fearful
was she, reversed, who couldn't speak without

seeming terribly alone. You see
we saw the terrible place from where
this sadness grew. A mobile home, a point
on the map, all of her children angry,
fighting for something better: the green fields,
the beaming moon and stars under Our Lady's feet.

Cotton Train, Ramsey Co., Minnesota

I didn't know the name of the flat-car ferrying
drunks between townships. It was sunset and the only things
alive that evening were brown faces against rust. Red wine
from their mouths like cheap blood. A dirty farmhand wishing
he were elsewhere. His manos like burnt meat or worse.
Clearing fields all day. Asleep now next to the Sioux
who keeps trying to get away from the res
where his sister's dying of TB: the train into Wisconsin

wishes them away. It doesn't sing to them
or play guitar. They might be known. Their faces might mean
love or endurance somewhere else. Unfastened
from the earth, they ride the pure hum of raw cotton
left clinging to the tracks. And when the sun makes miracles
of their bodies they count the rows they've cleared,
those yet to be undone.

H. Is Conquered and then Ignored

Panic & beautiful the end of your day,
when with love in their fists
new bearded strangers came pounding
far distances to see you, to be with you
maker of heaven. The dark sky
your brother who warned us in the year
12-house to fill our temples with gold
and the limp bodies of our enemies to make
holy on the feast day when these strangers arrived
smart and in the warm light shining
sweating men from another dimension.

H. Is Bound and Stripped

You know it began wet, your dreams all
flesh one morning—brother, it's always
the end of winter in Minneapolis.
Works no longer that Romeo
technology, that dry old shoe she left
here forty years ago, record album
with her voice. So they take you at midday,
& in custody you vomit, the glass

darkened sun a hot bonnet bursting
you back to the corner of your brain,
the naked stars nothing, your skull
& your hands nothing, you thinking of love,
how it was like that spring before when you
were blind to the comet shaving heaven for good.

Animal Time

I cut loose the last rope, my way back home
when we were all lambs and we were all born.
Between the animal meat and my brain
I let go in sunlight: there was a father
in all of this, speaking a dull language
with his dry tongue until the sun goes out
blue smoke filling the animals again.
I'll admit I don't know him, his back,

or his fine neck curving toward heaven—
in the evening when the thick trees turn black
and I am left to my body, slowly
the night rushes my mind to flame
and I cannot count the shuffling stars,
the holy holies who guard wicked doors.

La Invención del Televisor

Según Huitzilopochtli

He'll kill you if you whisper to the priest.
But in the garden behind the altar
he sits, the blue flickering of his dream
like the firefly he's crushing between
two fat fingers. For hours now he's painted
his lover's face with its electric juice:
because of the war that starves their children
they're awake and with their boredom take

the last pleasure from their bodies home
like something stolen or alone. It's here
he invents the first set, a radio,
later that first beautiful machine tuned
impossibly to all our frequencies,
to each heart on the continent, a gift.

On the Edge of Space, H. Speaks of the Infinite Void

The moon is a dream best attained in sleep:
filled with electricity and longing
like the last warm minutes of the day,
like a design on the lawn from the deep
oak rising in the shadows. What follows
is nothing but starlight. To desire
the crepuscular is an infinite
leap to the grave equilibrium where
the sun has no effect. Spinning this way

you'll find my trail in the sky—
when crossing guesses off your map,
I become a bed-hot ember to you.
Remember—it's dark out there, and heathens abound.
No beliefs will satisfy these chiefs, who through
this infinite void roam but seldom roar.

To His Lords and Agents in the Field

It's all been like a grubby spring day.
Those early flowers are the tulip voices
who visit me on occasion after I leave
the bus and float like an angel to my job.
In some of the buildings they pipe in Brahms,
the piano's whole notes breaking
into the elevator car
like clarion stamens fixing the air.

This is the time of painted blue secretaries
explain to me the end of the fifth world
and what it means to work in this fine city
of the apocalypse—the papers we pass contain
words tongued by a god whose voice is the deep
flute C-note whose emblem is everywhere, blameless.

"De las Diez Estrellas que Encontré, Tres Me Hablaron: Las Otras, Se Fueron en Vapor."

You are touching someone you barely know
comparing her shoulders to the angel Gabriel's
in the hallway of a shop your father's
owned since the Depression. It's love you feel
for the warm clothing she's folded next
to the stove. But you're from Tejas. Maybe
because it's nearly two in the morning
you know what it's like: foolishly treading ice.

God is with you and with the cowgirl
parting her legs. It's Saturday night—all
the thieves have gone down to the dance.
So when her mother comes looking for her
you're both up in a cottonwood tree, stealing
the sky, any weak stars in your favor.

Byzantine Comments of an Uncertain Nature:

The Martyrdom of St. Botolph

December again: all the lonely men
You know have fled Boston for Santa Barbara or Tucson.
Upstairs you mutter *who is this enemy,*
what time! It's right now, it's always right
now that you run your eyes past the old scars
of deadbolt locks ruining your bedroom door—
the next room needs her thighs, the next room needs your light!
Something about the way she doesn't shine.

December again: all the pretty bedspreads
Lined up for her to buy. On a walk to Newbury
empty she seem'd, evading all thy thrusts—
O she's a virgin you'll chart earlier! You're so blind,
now so literally blind, the smartest among you dead,
the enemy floating above your dirty head.

El Espejo Fumeroso

She knew a mirrored twin, began to write
small letters, notes really, in patient script.
He'd then reply with a story about his body,
the hidden left-side liver,
how he died when doctors couldn't find
his sick appendix. But naturally
he came back, urged by the black spot
growing on his heart, that fine muscle
tuned against his nature.
After a while, though, it's all up to the heart, she'd say.
Who's to know the smoke tasted delicious,
that children roamed his hallways? It was when he was alive
with the black desert sky that he forgot
her letters, useless now but understood
in the back-draft as he counted his way
past the minor planets lining heaven.
Words were everywhere those days,
sullen reminders lifting the faithful to new
intersections. It was with these holy
engines he found her, a flashlight shining
with her pulse, a compass point directed
into his body where he felt her skin,
the fine throb of her wet temples humming
and the taste of her mouth.
His mirror surrounded by her mirrors.
The truth: his arrows flew right,
her fractured kin welcomed him back home.

H. Sings the Catechism: A Chicano Rap Version at the Gates of a Small Cemetery Outside Hatch, NM, September 1991

Let's see: nací en El Paso, Tejas,
pues crecí en Albuquerque, en los suburbios.
He tenido una vida de trampas,
y cuando estudié en la universidad,
varias mujeres me jodieron.
I lived una vida menor and now I think
I'm in heaven waiting for God to speak.
When the men folk are finished turning

And their cheeks are burning with the calm
ash of forgotten cousins I'll take my place
carry her coffin to the tall gray poplars
that are forever reaching from the desert
toward a yellowed, Mexican moon
on the other side of the highway, this graveyard.

In the City of Smoking Mirrors

The future is a cartoon of the future.
I work downtown where the buildings are light as air.
Above me in the catalogue of floating streetlamps
the wind was turning the steam of the power station to ice.

I work downtown where the buildings are light as air:
Once I saw the perfect reflection of the rest of the city.
The wind was turning the steam of the power station to ice.
It was a clear blue afternoon and geese were returning north.

Once I saw the perfect reflection of the rest of the city
in one woman's dark eye as she window-shopped in front of Saks.
It was a clear blue afternoon and geese were returning north.
She loved the reflections of passing birds in the sky.

In one woman's dark eye as she window-shopped in front of Saks
the whole world opened and the cracks radiated to heaven.
She loved the reflections of passing birds in the sky.
The light stayed late and she thought of late winter:

the wind was turning the steam of the power station to ice
above me in the catalogue of floating streetlamps.
I work downtown where buildings are light as air.
The future is a cartoon of the future.

2.

I must now speak to my disciples, west

and east. I say to you, do not delay,

I say, expectation is vain.

—John Berryman, *The Dream Songs*

After Reading a Verse from the Holy Quran, Huitzilopochtli, in the Autumn Light to His Young Scribes Explains the Overwhelming Event

It's in amazement I write to tell you about space, not where the
    stars dwell
but rather where we live among the tall pine, sycamore and
    dogwood.
I can never tell you how to *feel*—it's up to you to notice
the mad look in my eyes the television gave me, the look
I use to greet the businessmen and bureaucrats in hell.
And about the bombing: the souls who roasted
will not dwell in my little heaven but will rest
on calm blue sheets, loved and nourished by coyote's own great
    teats!

You see, not believing now is worse.
The demons you'll have to defeat on your inward journey
are like so many little yellow hornets buzzing about
window screens in summer, angry but looking
for anything sweet, any way out—in the wild fields
outside groaning, in the ash-cans and offices roaming.
Every morning, you see, I fuck a wild woman while roses
swirl around her head: it's then I hear the live oak
singing in winter as her breath becomes mine—
O that we're so careless as the trees
to leave our clothing behind.

The overwhelming event asks us to reconsider
the teleological message written into its occurrence:
there's a prayer book with all our names in it somewhere,
the hymns we know written down neatly in pencil
by the original hand that guided Lot away from Sodom.

So here we are in this room without windows,
the insects going mad. If only we could break
into little groups to find our own truth, the
Womb's truth, the Lamb's truth. Even the truth
of some wounded blackboard from another century
that never slips in its dusty conveyance of order to you or me.

H. Writes to His Brother to Assure Him of Continuous Comfort in the Afterlife

Now comes upon us North Star, O smoking
mirror I invoke your charge, brother from
the laudanum sustaining us all. From my visions pray
for us now the war's begun. Healed not,
our hot blood nation rises dear, secret
weapons never used before against children—
the cleft mountain, that green plain you dream of
shattered so no Buddha would come to sit,

no decent man would take his children near.
Brother twin, the advice I give is like
a deep icy breath taken in a snowstorm:
I can't tell you what it's like to love, or
how to court the young natives so they
open gladly arms leading to the inevitable kiss.

Now comes the truth of winter we think. Our
enemies who hold the bomb mean to burn
us all: you & me, the gardens we've planted
in this life, so far. And now, with the One
European God watching from another
galaxy, a far-out thought I have is that
the music will end, we'll find ourselves
in Mixtlán among the dogs, swimming for

sandy shores somehow reminding us of home:
the girls were easy. Blue turquoise eyes,
favorite birthstones, scientist's daughters all.
Just help me as the next life begins in
some suburb or another, coasting clear
of fathers who don't want to know our names.

La Chota Frega a Huitzilopochtli en el Camino

Puercos azules oíganme:
I'll no longer pray for you
in the weak morning
light of the cathedral.
Descúlpenme en el suelo,
like the bright woman who pieces
the eyes of Jesus together
when the moon is a slice of light
and speaks lies, all lies.
Les dije que no soy su amante:
ella me invita como los ecos que otros han dejado.
It's a poor trick to predict love.
It'll only call back the duendes
from the thick stands of cottonwood
to visit with you in the cellar
of your prairie home.
Puercos azules mírenme:
I am going to scrape
your hearts tonight through
an etherous dimension
and our skins will stink of asphalt.
Cuando estemos en el otro lado
llorarán los rincones del mundo,
llorarán las tetas de las mujeres bravas,
their invincible children who will
seek any hope now that the stars are sick,
and losing to the ocean.

A Story from Colorado Days

It's in the afterlife—your children
growing high as pines, my children
off on some planet mining new poems, new songs—
the story I'm telling old enough to be wrong:
Bear, it was in one kitchen we sat waiting to score, the clock
like a tin rooster ticking, the linoleum-covered table
glad to have us. And so when the bud arrived
we left, telling each other to read the other's
light-bulb dreams, whichever came first, a story
here or there in the ether, a story you might think of
driving in the dark mountains of southern Colorado
when the wind had started in from the Northwest
and there was nothing but darkness in that sky.
Bear, dreaming now in my winter exile,
where the war has come and sewn itself into all our lives,
O, I had no idea we'd be here—
watching the icy road between our pueblos,
squatting over the ashes other humans have left,
drawing designs in the water-drowned
fire that once cast light on everything, even
beyond the stars beginning to shine
in the lackadaisical darkness above our dirty heads.
Bear, I must end this note by telling you
we made it home to Alamosa, there for me to smoke
the last remains of a dried flower the old graybeard gave me,
flower that caused so much trouble, caused me to sing,
brings me to your little town to hear about the past, anything
at all to conjure life from my still drying bones.

Minor Hints of a Legacy of Sorrow and Pain

You're the stranger who comes once a month to dine.
And when you walk the back streets
you can taste one man's supper
as it steams the kitchen windows
behind where he sits admiring the warmth:
there's light pouring through
and his face is a suburban half-moon
lighting his house with the reflections
of a dead satellite spinning in darkness.

So he fills your plate.

And when your hunger finally dies
the table he saved for you to sit at
he chops to kindling, sets out
for local boys to cart away:
small fires are placed in every greasy doorway
where you've eaten,
your path to the grand oblivion
of skyscrapers, a bright maze
where your heart, doused in prophecy, will falter.

Brujo Leaving Hawthorne's Woods,

New England, 1995

For your body I cut
a length of cottonwood from a crooked tree.
It grew along the Rio Grande
and the smell of it burning excited the duendes
living in the small closet next to the fireplace—
where I kept the kindling, chips of wood I saved
from last season. When I owned a house
in Colorado the spirits taught me
to cook bark in a red pot, to leave hot grease
under the elms at noon when I wanted them to speak.
That and to spit three times into the snow
when ravens flew overhead.

For your soul I chewed
corn husks and bear-grass, the result
I buried in the earth. And every night
I fumbled with my rosary, trying to forget
the false magic my grandmother taught me.
Last week, burning at night with a sickness from the stars
I wrote a poem about the drunks in Silver City, NM
who drink blue Aqua Velva when they're too poor for Tokay—
under a black sky they wait for the planets to rise,
they wait for the dark buzz to take them
to the same small places you'll never name.

Five Dollars

The upper Midwest unrolls under me.
I'm still anonymous in one of the larger cities
rising from the plain like the ghost of a dead buffalo
entering the cusp of native heaven: the grass is so high
in places as to permanently hide from a man all his tools,
the rudiments of farming and civilization. In this sea
I'm wrecked, anchored in one of the old suburbs of steam and
    snow.

Near the end of the millennium
the Beatles are on the radio. It hardly matters
the terrible violence overtaking this century
settles like the new gray song they've put together.
For more life, or the promise of secular advancement,
their song plays all the time. From what I've heard
it reminds the stellar suburbanites of the fine pulse
Lennon felt when he went down. It was winter in New York
and his life was a movie. It's winter now

in the dim downtown where I've taken five dollars
to spend. The last time I was here
a jogger saw me getting stoned. That's all this life requires.
To fall in love with the few who'll look my way,
a nod of acquaintance, or finally
a grasp and tug away from this brief world. Like a commuter
I'll start sleeping on the bus, outbound toward
the yawning family homes that glow like charcoals in the twilight.

Letter from H. to the Faithful Who Await His Communiqués in Some Dim Future

Compas, in my dream America is poor
and at Christmas families sit on their porches
playing hearts. There is no more winter.

So when the heat finally dies
the timeless distance where you live
will betray your endless patience for me,
lovers of letters predicting your future:

you'll smell the perfume of my many
consorts who bared their backs to the desert,
to park benches and grasses now burned beyond recognition.

You'll feel my heart sinking in your mouth
like a blue plum. And over your shoulders,
in the mirror where my brain shines
into another dimension

somewhere in New England, the sea reaching toward me
like a hungry hand, the tourists who walked there one summer
sleeping in cold blue rooms

fists clenched between their thighs.
Tonight when I count the stars
of my heaven I'll think of you,

the great yellowed rooms you inhabit,
the small stories of me you share
standing around your fires and your books.

A Letter to My Brothers and Sisters in North Korea

Where will all the music go if you bomb us?
Do the fashion magazines lie?
I hate to be serious, North Korea.
There are stations playing all night here, though,
and sometimes the disc jockeys spin
old dreams of love
Almost no one gets, awkward frequencies
announcing us to the stars.

I've heard many of you
starving in railway stations.
Your cobbler-sick hue
won't keep me from calling you.
And I don't have apples.
There's no way the TV stations could lie.
Your cobbler-sick hue
won't keep me from calling.

North Korea, in one of my magazines
there's a girl without shoes. In one of my tea cups
a .30-caliber bullet, an indescribable lotus
blossom wrapped crudely in wax.
It's for when you cross the sea
in your rocket
with the thousand-petaled sun
so bright, so bright.
But before that happens
I'm calling your sons and daughters
and I'm gonna tell 'em
the evil red communism
never happened here

we're happy watching beautiful
models and basketball players
the evil red communism

failed here and will always fail
here because we have the Dodgers
we have supermarkets
we have lovely green rooms
under the Rockies
where our warriors sleep
in their own slow radiation.
But that argument has ended, too.

Sadly and terribly
atoms conspire against us
generals conspire against
all of my favorite songs
keep us from knowing
our bodies, our hands
how we could mingle
or touch under blankets.

Radios are a must, North Korea.
For if I choose to love you
anymore, with your winter
hats made of coyote fur,
and the children you drop off at the zoo,
I'll have a song in my head
for all of your dead, that's all for you,
a gift from the stars

that sounds almost new.

Discovering a Christian Hymnal

In the suburbs
I read a cruel pamphlet.
Its gray cover
announced safety in basements.

I read it with a girl one afternoon.
She believing in Christ stopped—
our explorations stopped,
revealing millions asleep
under the suicide sky. That night

the air was unhealthy,
cars and chimneys choking out
the invisible monoxide, citizens
singing Yuletide at the grocery store.

I imagined miles up
swarms of winter sparrows
returning to Mexico.

In the desert beyond Arroyo del Oso
boys rode up to bonfires on dirt bikes.
They warmed their hands
and drank from a shared
bottle of whiskey stolen that morning.

In the hills
developers with names like
falling branches were building
new homes daily. Whole families
grew up in subdivisions

unafraid of the desert, not knowing
the shell sky is an upturned tin mirror frame.

Anyone leaving his house
would not be lonely. Strangers
quickly began to understand:
the new shadows of swallows
arrived while the neighbors turned
their soft voices
to each other like radio announcers.
They didn't know the dark
animal of loneliness speaking through them,
the constellations tumbling into morning.

Huitzilopochtli to His Children in the Year 2032

There are no strange songs on my radio
as the third millennium plays out
in one suburb after another.
And the watery light of winter waters

each of our gardens and we find ourselves
muttering words—melodies sweep old poems
clear of dead moorings. There's even a poet
singing on the phonograph this morning:

the slow brass band swinging in the background
is the only indication of a world
beyond his vinyl-garbled words. Still,

he is telling us to be brave, to love
the underwater lights, the stray phrases
he conjures from his unapproachable dreams.

Downpour

Chartered to tell the truth,
he went out seeking
those who ate the sepia of memory with him.

1.

There's a song
weaving itself into the afternoon—
for years the neighbors
didn't listen and the tune
flowed at three pm like water.
The air was an arroyo,
the salt cedars canals.

Now in the scorpion desert
the drumming in the distance
is the city unfolding itself to rain.
The pounding is your heart, and is
thought to be a spirit seeking
this world.

In the foothills
neighbors pull their curtains
tight across daylight: heat vanishes,
shade is loved for qualities
spoken of only at nightfall, when faces
ignite under the gaseous stars.

2.

The best days
beckon like salt.
Rested, I still howl,
grappling with my bones,
finding chalk. The sacred
heart doesn't rest here.

Or consider
the animal of our creations
lying in the grass. Her smooth
hair ruins many. To duplicate
her endeavors is a failure of faith.

Lying in the grass
the smooth leaves cut
the back of my head
and whisper. In summer
I hide, oat blind.

3.

I am no carpenter,
having cut my
fingers at the saw.
Your voice
fills the page.

I do not know you.
I ride the air, exchanging
ghost songs.

This is the muse
who loves blood
pudding and salt.

The Dry Oak Leaves Burning Like Myrrh

One time in Hawthorne's woods
Coyote and I sat with two old storytellers who fed us clams &
    bread pudding.
Afterward, we listened to the Beatles—Bear, I swear our hosts
    marveled
At how we sang like John or George, & in the whiskey haze
discovered we that light curiously bent around all of us,
the angelic light of New England shining in the kitchen window.

Bear, the light of Eastern Wisconsin falling
over the St. Croix this frosty morning
is like the first burst of autumn on a county highway—
right now the neighbors are burning oak leaves in the alley,
& the morning sun is meeting the quarter moon
for the second time in two months.
From my bedroom window, warmth's just beginning to fall on
me.

Re-born under the astronomic double cleavage of surrender that
    morning
the first thing I named was her body, that river
I met in the delta, immune traveler from the stars.
My dear correspondent, the half-life of my heart lasted
only so long, the resonance of a recorded song.

O Bear, I ache to sing in the dry forest
I ache to build huts of white pine & mud
to sleep safely all winter, dreaming of salmon and the wide sky.
Only so long. When Coyote & I pack our things into a truck,
drive West with our children sleeping between us,
I'll call so loud, I'll yell, I swear.

H. Writes His Dead Amigos for the Sake of Clarity

I will be with you again—our dogs running
in the piñon hills outside of Gallup, New Mexico, until sunset.
Nightly then, fat lamb steaks
or mutton stew and warm tortillas, the snow
march to the hot springs where bared to the stars
we'll talk all night of Proust or Hesse, we'll trade
sly homoerotic looks under the moon,
who, in washing our backs in light absolves us of any wrong.

Primarily, my lords,
the poems in the lost manuscript contained
a suppressed history of Dinetah as felt through the heart
of Dear Brother Begay, lost to us in alcoholic fire.
It was the witch of the south who in her bitterness took
flight with these words, these typed pages hacked out
one drunken morning in Albuquerque, to save
in a wooden box made from saw-ruined hands.

I will begin with you, amigos, whom I left on the roadside
long ago, walking away into the green, flowering hills
to live my life of hallways, children, and smoke—
where I live the northern sky hides everything
from me, near-sighted astronomer cosmonaut
who now must wander the boreal wilderness instead!
O, I still let my one dog roam the woods for any hint
of your kingdom—the black crows gathering,

the amethyst sky in January dusk.
Every tired moment I walk in the gray winter woods
my lords, it is for your presence that I long—while no
two men can be friends if they love the same woman, I pray
in the spirit world that our hounds and terriers

will cross that long bridge to find us
like warriors advancing on the dead hills to Mixtlán—holding
     hands,
singing savage songs to give us hope as we face the south wind.

The Far Subdivisions

1. Desert Landscape

The forgetful snow of desert mantras
unfolding like little prayer books brought me here.
I couldn't sleep
under the yellow street light guarding my home
so I walked a distance into the desert,
snow squalls shifting overhead in meditation
to the warmer ground. I was blessed.
It was the end of the year and the last neighbor
turned off his lights. In every house a fire burned
the heart sick, the dull remains
of new year drifting in the air like smoke.
Alone on the new sidewalk couples tipped glasses
and as I walked house to house, the great blue light
of TV commanded a corner in each. Essentially,
I had a burning in my mouth causing prophesy.
I called each bastard to his door
in a native tongue I couldn't master
but blustered out in grunts. They didn't hear me.
Detained in reverie their bodies never moved.

2. He Dreamed of the Devil

In the half-light of mesquite trees dying in winter
I dreamed a dance in a dry field—
my father's family hung tin lanterns,
and a conjunto played rancheras
from the bed of a pickup truck.
My mother told me the devil was there.
She saw his bright hooves reeling.
In the dark, under a table, his hands were claws
grabbing her sister's thighs.
He said he'd carve my chest,
reveal the last secret
I've buried there.

3. The Accident

Over and over, before he lost his body to the snow,
what was more important than heaven to a floundering man
were the thick layers of the world he saw dying.
His mouth was filled with water and his face
would color the TV news for days. His ugly black
moustache like the broom they used
to brush the snow away. His heart
a thick blue muscle. I could hear him scream
in my sleep. He didn't know me or the bright
angel who sat by my bed to count the scars in my mouth.
They were all laughing at the stories I told.

4. The Great Depression

The country's stretched us thin.
Because I haven't worked in weeks
my mind lacks proper definition.
I'm sick. In the cities men
feed off the cooling grunts of steam
left falling into the sky. I know one
who'll cut you up and toss you to the wind.
He's breathing the hot gases released
from heating ducts, from plumbing. He's listening
to the rustle of skirts and onionskin.
On the radio his voice recalls
the contracts cut in hell's blue ink.

5. In Transit

To be transient these days is like a forge:
the force and delight of metal compares
to the burn of faces that sickens my hours.
This adventure has reduced itself to an odd note,
a deer slowly grazing at the end of winter.
To be in love with brown August petals,
things in the sky, is odd, beyond replacement.
Yet burned or worried we arrive every morning
ready for warm food.

In the gray evening house by the river
we met and commented on the shapes of trees,
what we saw nightly in the sky, windows
framing these bright comets and new discoveries.
We danced to waltzes and contracted love from
the freshly mown hay thrown to the floor!
Dear reader, the train is filling, bags rumble
through empty corridors. When we have slept five hours
porters will wake us with tales of limes
cut from the cables above us.

6. The Violence of Machines

Pulled from the lips
and hips of thin women
I gaze open-handed.
Taken for love
my heart is large
from drinking whiskey.
The violence of machines
at times twists my hands, my knuckles.
It is not that I do not trust your arms or habits.

One afternoon in March
I crossed into a ditch,
rang the bells of another belief:
what the rain split in me
the traveled river road undid. First
my skin escaped me, finally
the heart-water drained.
What I dug that day from the mountain loam
I carry daily, the name of a field.

3.

From the shore of death you can see the stars better.

—Carlos Fuentes, *The Orange Tree*

H. Writes to Bear after Looking into a Muse's Uncertain Eyes

From this life I've stolen the feathers
of the ruby-throated hummingbird
to line Plutonian shores. Away
from here the sun cooks space and nothing
I know is not cold, not cloak-wrapped
stellar nonsense, fluttering atoms.
Right across from where I'm working
obscene poets are figuring the doom
of things—you know, burning cities,
callous children dancing in the ashes of their books.
But for me, dear Bear, the theological
moment has already happened. No bombs
only issues that turn out like little
cacti on the desert floor.

Now it's time to call in our aces,
to put our long fingernails into grinding wheel.
I hope from this to prophesy the next twelve hundred years—
your sleep my dear Bear will keep you fat and dreaming of the
    wide
glittering sky awaiting your dawn. Think of it:
fruit and the impossible whisper of life when you return.
Calling you from the boreal wilderness, after all,
will be me, who knows all the evils of the world,
who cries and cannot sleep. And because I have too much need
for innocence I'll wake you into the new heavenly
world to give us all the sweet presence of your company,
to remind us of those quiet dinner times
when the hard dry walnuts were all we ate, were all.

Manifest of a Boat Leaving on the Eve of
the Third Millennium

In one satchel you'll be carrying newsprint, comics dark
with vegetable ink, the faces drowned, unknown.
At your feet a box filled with placards,
your name, your family's, pictures you're not to discuss.

When history collapses in the suburbs, every family
will weep constantly for their personal god to come screaming
in the door, hands full of new credit cards. On the lawn
lonely messengers await, wings drawn so far
into their bodies you'll think they're human.
Take their instructions. Commit them to your notebook:

If you believe the books, the world should've ended by now.
But the sky hasn't turned itself off yet. What used to be the tears
of a giant whose name we forgot waters prairies, vast sandy
    oceans
we can never cross. For fear of dying. Or worse.
To see others like you or me burning in the abhorrent sun
draining out sweat, our fat tongues salty.

Out here in winter's whirl
We're crafting another memento. It takes the place
of all those lost TV transmissions, the sad voices
of radio announcers the future won't get to know.
While those comfortable voices jaunt to unknown stations

we'll be counting the static of souls
left aching in the malls, in a thousand highway rest stops.
We'll want to know each one
before climbing up the twisting Manila-rope ladder, home.

A Dark Book of Painful Years

That black river had washed my body enough—
the shallow banks of salt cedar
along the irrigation ditch leading from a well
were like rows of houses in any abandoned suburb.
It's home, near the water where we bathe
and the children bathe.
On New Year's Day neighbors saw me
crawling on the side of the road
hunting for the small deer mouse
that bit my boy on the finger.
Fearful of rabies and the sore end
of my hijo's finger swelling
like a balloon into the twenty-first century
I looked under all the pine needles,
up to the sky where a radioactive god
will eat us and taste on our skin
the dirt, all the dirt under our nails.
We were digging the children's graves
we were digging the mothers' graves
we were burying the books and the radios.
And now I'm lonely for the suburbs,
the unused dishes and wine glasses that are lonely—
the grass grows over all of us,
chronicling like a film our neat shadows
that are like fine cinders in a cold hearth,
and the wind talks to us at night.
It says *do not forget me hijos,*
do not forget the warm mouths,
the kisses you've left behind.

The One True Wound of Saint Robert Plutonium

In the bunker we hunted down each other's fears
until the radio came on. Thereafter in the only room with windows
I watched as winter morning seared the white walls blue—

once a day drift by the many dead, who in coming home from heaven
are like little brown sparrows. And just beyond the telephone poles
this city's glow in atomic radiation super advertising dust
destroys the plains, all the small towns miles out.

We traveled here and it was like a movie—
how the bright world slid into darkness on slick rails!
At each other's cheeks we watched the country go by.
And when the TV came back on

well, forget it: my thoughts were filtered by a sound
coming through the walls. It was called annihilation in a book
about the bomb I had,
and by the birds, who fewer now, surmount the lips of my reality.

Even now as the one God sleeps
he seems to be saying: eat, grow in the dust,
tell this story when you're old.

A Last Passage through Tucson

Little carpenter, little fox, how you
wandered from box to box quoting Cicero,
taking time to admire the Tucson sunset
from your adobe house on 5th. You always
came back over and over like the grackle
whose name you adore. But it's the future now
and stupidly, we're naked & in this
dream you're dead, weeping to me about

your heart, how it beat you when you followed me
from house to house. Me, I say, I'm waiting
for the one night when the sky is clear over
the boreal shores of Lake Nokomis—
this oaken kingdom I've claimed up north soothes
every passage down, from the desert once removed,
back to the burnt-out town whose single business
is to survive the heat. Pass through there again,

the pain will quicken, always.
Wood carver, painter, I fear we'll never talk this way:
I can't invite you to play, I can't ask you to conjure fevers
so I'll dream of prickly pear and saguaro. All I know
is there's no place in the sky we're going, and unlike
the gods we'll not dwell forever in the constellations.
Carpenter, passage of the heartless past,

O heart of stone whose burrow charms everyone
with books, with tea and scones, little carpenter,
you rose from box to box escaping boredom.
And like the night birds here, called only
in the deepest night when the moon was down,
when I began to lose your chiseled heart
among the tinder, the dark red chips I'd saved for winter.

On Finding His Friend Trickster Rabbit Crippled
from a Fall

Now that I live up north, exiled from the sharp
unforgiving prickly pear cacti growing in Grandmother's yard,
now that I know not its fruit nor the way ravens gather by the
    thousands
along the Rio Grande in October, only now
will I cry and cry to the electronic winds
that have taken me to you.

For no reason one day a murder of crows,
black, dead-squirrel-eating business fresh
shook me from my forest path—the largest yelling with the rest,
followed me through the oak and sycamore,
warning me of rain. O rabbit, you know
how quickly the summer wanes in Minnesota,
how the boreal forest wastes no time in claiming
anything dying. So when I walk through my little
23-acre kingdom and when I hear my sweet
children sing every morning
I know I will not outlast the sun.

I grow, like the old philosopher, mad by my own
calculations and investigations. Knowing nothing
new in the world I cannot ache for death or the love
of a transcendental moment in the woods that will free me
from all the sour prayer books that fill my mind.
Illusion, dear fellow, is like that day in class
when the little old schoolmaster knew we had him beat,
that all his songs we'd taken from him and somehow made better.

Dictionary of the Mad Sailor Guadalupe Trujillo

Once dreaming about the Mexican shore
off Puerto Peñasco, how there'd been
no city until the gringos
built a port for the war, I turned
aside the boat I rowed and began this book—
I can't tell you anything about the sea, other than
it's really green some nights
when the boys are out casting their nets
for shrimp and tuna. Already
I awake into your world, though.
My first entry is the abstract depiction
of the world. I mean a review
of color, the masses of brown
peoples shifting in and out of focus.
I awake into your world
and see your dirty pipe on the windowsill.
So my second entry is the blind
instrument you play, a flute
you say the devil gave you.
I awake into your world and
daylight's here, having arrived
like mild thunder stealing
the air, no body, impossible.
Daylight's here, having arrived
and I awake into your world—
the city's behind me, the last tuna boats
over the horizon have tuned to perfect frequencies,
groups of men listening for fish to glide
by their green and yellow nets.
We cleaned up when I was young. The
fish in droves scattered under our boats
like daylight. They awoke into our world
and fed the children who used to sell

burritos on the shore to tourists.
The third entry therefore
is the mad pain of poverty
that I endured that they all endure
behind the harbor, the seashell
streets or the beer shacks where
college kids congregate on Saturdays
when the sun is hot and the waves
are an ocean blue that'll kill you.
I awake into your world
after dreaming of the same pure
roads all over Middle America,
the dull hotel rooms where Coca-Cola salespeople
sleep with their cell phones turned on.
It's all so incomplete. So sure
we'll die, so sure we'll all die
I awake into your world with this warning:
when you take my book to the sea
in the morning, when you tear the cap
off a sacred Mexican mushroom, chew
slowly, more slowly than the slowest worm.
Before you read the introduction
the sky will fail, and when you die
you'll always wake into the same world—
the seawall's backed into a crisis tide,
thus the fourth entry I etch with the deliberate
stroke of a stonecutter—the story so far:
you've rowed with me to the empty sea
and alone we sleep in a wide canoe.
When I awake into your world we're facing starvation,
thirst. The book, now filled with incantations
nests between us. You know between its leather cover
there's nothing for us. So we'll die
out here, staring at each other's feet,

scribbling bad last entries when the sun goes down.
In the old days we'd steal the life of a gull
to stay alive, drink its meager blood, maybe
steer into a sea turtle leading its school
to shore. How the meat would taste, so red
so red, filling our mouths, filling our guts.
When I started writing again
I made my next entry, the fifth.
The dumb sun burned, we ate the last of the fish
and then saw gulls afterward—
we were out three days, making land
at la Isla de Bocas. In my hand I took the knife
and sliced the last rope holding
the boat, and we were alone on that wide island.
But we must get mystical again: out of paper
my last words were like the stars every night,
and knowing I would reach them soon I prayed
to the wide blue god above. My body,
my fruit, the last word had been shaved
from my head, had taken root in what you'd call
words, those strange syllables containing me,
all I'd become on this coconut island. It's not
that I refused to drink, but took my water all from God,
started rowing south to suit my sad reactions,
all I lost that summer to be somewhere found, somewhere found.

A Visit to the Hot Springs in the Sangre de Cristo Mountains

Who knew about the war, dear Bear?
You'd done battle with a rattlesnake
in the Sonoran Desert south of Tucson
hardly knowing about the northern springs that feed
a whole resort for naked Anglos to worship
each other in oaken tubs shipped from colonized Japan.
Yet you saw the anthrax form
on American lips sometime before
that awful conflict started. That story you wrote
while I bathed high in the post-colonial New Mexican
wilderness was like the serotonin-soaked rich girl whose nudity
in the piñon hills merely startled us.
What I saw that night was the last snake dream
I had in the desert waiting for my lover to emerge from the earth.
Somewhere in the water the image
bubbling out was the new world drifting
away into the cold air above Santa Fe—
now the war builds engines greater than love,
now we must fight in the air above, faith
pinned to our radiation-hardened sleeves.

Una Compañera del Norte

Se la encontró el H.—era del árbol, era de la mano izquierda
también. It was all well and good that scraping
the floors one summer there'd be some reflection
proving to H. he really lived in someone else's curled
series of dreams, and while he might not know
the color of sheets this dreamer forever rolled in,
he might hear the sound of oaks whipping
in the summer rain, above someone's head.
Ves: beside her lovely house
it was like a fairy tale because the good-willed
stream had brought him to a series of inner-connected
rooms reminiscent of Dr. Einstein's stripped-out
brain on a table at Princeton awaiting a final probe
at its mysterious genius. The case was this—
some doppelgänger! A twin who dressed like him
and paused from room to room to wonder
if what she saw was a mechanical rendition of her life—
a teacher of small children who forever kept
picture books in her backpack, endearing herself to H.
who couldn't see sometimes his eyes burned from searching
so many texts for any word of the next life.
But what he called the future was galloping his way
like a tide of insensate horses caught up
in the clear dry air of perfect Mongolia.
What couldn't be made up
was the long summer solstice evening when for the first time in
    years he saw
as many stars as he could, standing shoulder to shoulder
with an old demon friend who had chased him out
of the desert and into the cold northern forests.
Without H. to sting, that little yellow whip slipped back

into the night, rode home to the hot cinder-block walls of Phoenix
where he waits to clamber into the sheets
of sleepy drunks and potheads who've stopped
wearing shirts because of the heat.

The Circumnavigation of Hell

1.

It started early, the red sky boiling over the next county we
    wanted to spy.
I could see then the hot stones smoking on the ledge of a cauldron
in the high New Mexico hills where the warm springs ran
from the earth. So when I started walking it was east,
the wet road winding down to cornfields and humming
superhighways taking us through the night to Hell.
My guide was singing. A long time ago the Mexicans called her
Coyote—her red hair shone in the passing headlights hour
after hour until we reached a town somewhere.
We'd shaved our luck down by walking under Taurus, now
we ate in the shadows, searching the ground for signs,
cigarette butts that could tell us where to go.
She told me I was dead, that the river wasn't far away.
When I remember now I know we weren't breathing.
Fruit grew for us from the ground and finally from our flesh.
We crossed to the first level, soaked sometimes in blood
Like the oranges growing on my thigh.
We had no map so wandered through the hills eating this way,
days meaning nothing, we had no days or nights.
And when the ground hardened like winter on earth, we slept
    again—
there were animals to catch and eat. In Hell
the next circle lets you breathe again. So when my guide left me
for a bit I traced my way back to one young man I met who
    sinned
for no pure reason, who sat without hands in a rose garden
discussing the seasons. Frantically, there were no seasons.
Hell goes down and down toward ugly towns that boast of blood,
empty corners where no heart will pump, where no love will color
the gray habits of the dead. In one radiation-sickened hovel

you might find remnants of some long-lost lover, her letters,
a bowl of rotting pears. Again and again you hear there's
another boundary to cross, a war zone where sinners dig for food.
You see, I was back again on a field playing lover to Coyote.
She whisper'd near enough my heart to make me turn inside
like I was living. I could hear chafing grass against her back—
there are new gods in Hell, and the stars turn on nothing.

2.

Some demon-traded secret in the room was making me write.
Outside the white sky baffled Coyote, who dressing stood
under the light so I could see her wan face wake—
we were home but in someone else's dream, a motel in the Mojave,
a black scorpion skittering across the kitchenette's linoleum.
Was it the 1950s? We hunched by listening for a vague tone
on the telephone to tell us we were home. There was light
on this level, but made by a devil who sat with his thick legs
crossed on the top of a hill. Here he was a god to these dead who
    wandered
from one movie set to another, living only to die in violence:
a shoot-out, or sometimes an atomic bomb dropped from a North
    Korean plane.
It was all the same—these souls suffered
his wrath and were eaten, only to reappear in the next sequence,
whole and ready to be beaten. Blasted from this level we watched
from the air as the monster ate: picking a wretch he'd
strike a blow to the neck of his victim then dash the body
into his jaws. Sickened we dropped away to a land where
the dead live on Mars, sleeping in dry caves, immune to loneliness.
Remember, Hell is not all violence: there was a place we walked to
where the lotus blossoms grew, where thick stands of cannabis
flowered on the Martian plains while the dead tended fields of flax
and rose at dawn to watch the blue Earth slide by like an errant star.
I knew now Hell was episodic, that we might end up living
the cold war, that even Coyote was dead and just as dead as I was
not going back to my familiar bed in the morning.

3.

We were over the river. I discovered this world was made
from that river, Lethe, where dead poets fling what's left
of their verse into bags and sling these greasy sacks behind
the only gate to Pandemonium, hoping they'll be back
when Resurrection's trumpets sound and goodness conquers
    Satan.
But it's dark here and sharp stones cut back any progress toward
the cold hills. And my guide was all but gone, looking for
what was left of her heart. The body, not surviving
death becomes a figment of the imagination, a beauty
that'll not survive the inferno, the hatreds God pours out.
We left the last sinners spinning their sad stories in the sand
with twigs and broken pencils, anything they could find.
There was not Satan near, just the wan belief
we're not getting any better, that progress is a lie.
So when Coyote met me once again she had a story
of her travels without me: naked again she'd been
waiting to wake up in that bed she'd left so long ago—
the man she'd loved wasn't here and who knows
how time is lived on other planets? This wasn't quite Earth.
I knew all my friends were gone, or I was gone from the world of
    sunlight—
we know nothing of this thin dimension where we live
or sleep or slip into danger!
Mean maps mean little in the dark corners, when without shoes
    or courage
waded we into the fire, into the phosphorescent
underworld pools where the devils waited
to boil our souls like the small flying fish
Sailors catch when they're at the equator.
Two sights I've seen since I arrived: the red gates shining,
the air above it a pandemonium stretching for a hundred miles.
That and Coyote, who found me on a gray stretch of road
I'd thought was near my home. But I'd died out there walking.

So like any dead man at first I lost my breath until soft life went
    away.
Setting sights on unnamed stars, I walked until my hips were sore.
Then there was Coyote—a ride she offered
but only to Hell, a back way where we'd learn how to handle
    strange ropes
twisted from hemp and nylon—strange boats sailing for us.

4.

You may ask dear reader what bespoke of Hell's dim cast?
And I'll take you to a graveyard, under a colonial oak
where in October anyone can see falling to the ground
the green letters from summer quickly dying. Fast approaching
death like that, the voice of each leaf stifled under snow.
And so I lived with the trees. I lived in the ground and dug
the earth a home where I could sleep, where I could go if I feared
    life.
My dark past made me go astray, but I was not swayed by some
    dumb planet
fixed to the sun. I planned for pleasure and fame, I planned to
    claim
anyone who gave me love. I climbed into life and never wanted,
    then.
So when I died, the leaves, the bricks, the roads never went away,
or maybe the stuff of the world is always there,
written in between our lives. It didn't matter.
Having left the oaks I waited for Coyote.
Was she a girl I knew? Or another of the newly dead making her
    way down?
I knew her from the outset. Even before we were naked.
The bed I left that night to trod the road
was made of oak, a strong place for dreams—how her moonlit
    face
shown new & lovely. So Coyote reminded me
of every lover I'd known: something about the way she folded
her hands or how we waited now for boats to sling across the
    harbor:
that we might board these sleek ships, that we might sail for
    another home.
The final darkness isn't a pit that winds inside Satan's hairy belly.
It's another land that you or I might know, a land
cast and tilted toward futility, an empty paradise of bones

where the dead quiver in amazement at the loss they suffer.
With no bodies they inhabit the air, and uncentered, drift for ages
     alone.
In what place was my soul at such soft times? While I lived
another like me fought the ocean somewhere,
thoughtless and unaware of my life. How much is he in me
I cannot know, but flowing from my dreams are scenes of the sea,
a way I never knew in life. The taste of salted pork,
a young man bleeding to death under sparkling black skies.

5.

The hard ocean rose to meet the ship in green waves
and for a while we were swamped. Nothing out here lived
that wasn't part of the sea. Storms soon mocked us—we never
    slept
knowing how far we'd go to reach land. Waves, surf, rocks,
we'd swim for shore if we had to, no matter we might drown.
For in the distance on a small isle was a town where everyone was
someone from the past, where there were sweets and fast food,
warm burgers, thick drumsticks sweating grease, chocolate.
But because everyone is sick in Hell and demons of disease swirl
in the rusty air, once again, there is no hope.
Only the dream of islands offshore that beam their love skyward
to the dark satellites swimming overhead.
So we sailed, sleeping in the forecastle, retreating now and then
    topside
to overhear the cheating wind rubbing the sails with anxious
    gusts.
Otherwise, the sailors wouldn't let us out, but we the dead
would crowd around portholes when the boat slowed, when we
    rounded
a goodly stretch of shore where shone a black light
casting hopelessness everywhere.

These are their days: Odysseus brave still burns out there
skirting the southern shores for food, red-skinned now,
Odysseus without his tongue and filled with a hunger
for the tale he cannot tell, the end of his story.
You sight him at a distance, his boat
coasting the clear summer waves, this second Mediterranean
it's all become. The boys who sailed with him long ago
still rowing, awful in the jowls and forearms. Some of them
howl for lost Ithaca, knowing they've sailed to challenge only
starfish, tuna, blue whale. Anywhere the sea drops,

anywhere the stars are new every night yet close enough
to swell their stupid hearts. Those of us trying to touch
these clouded yellow bulbs are burned—for Satan is yours
surely on this boat, you are his new bride
overcoming the lights to reach his tasty shore.

6.

Unlost not again and sail sound I hunger for my life
the fleshy experience of skin on skin, the taste of anything ripe,
even dream I must of small, juicy plums, newly fallen.
My girls are gone and like an old father I drift between scenes,
what's etched on the edge of a magazine. Please, the song is over.
For when I sing anew it's with the chafe of galleon rows
I make my passage. Hard muscles now, piss later, the oars, the
    oars!
I know not the sea, but hear it crack the timbers.
The dead men behind me hiss—we've hit a shoal somewhere—
a whisper, then the pure silence of a still night,
the woes awaiting us in Antarctic waters.

Floating thusly, reader, I didn't sink but came to shore
on a cannibal island, and facing south could see the rim of Hell
curve in its hoary architecture home. I say cannibals although
each sinner with a particular meal ate what seemed to be
his own body, roasted and served on porcelain.
I wasn't walking here long without others. As in a game
we found a passage outward, signs on the wall of stars and minor
    planets
lining Heaven. My Coyote in a hallway sat still soaked
from the wreck, a map curled in her dirty hands.
There is no way but through the ambivalent air of purgatory,
and of the meetings with my demon I will tell you.

7.

Some say he's kind to me, allowing in my life a woman,
that wife who watches o'er me like an errant saint.
But of the nights when his darkness rules I know
only of his sublime order: the truth comes to me slowly.
Waking in this stunned dream my arms tingle—
he is at first the brave Huitzilopochtli, flower king who ebbs
from my dreams like a shrinking rose. His robes
are the flayed skins sacrificed for him, men and boys, humming-
    birds.
And knowing what it's like to be dead he touches
my naked head to begin: what occurs isn't sanctified
but a transmission of his diabolical mind to mine. No longer a man
there's nothing I need. But for a while I am his spirit,
a body possessed in your world, reader. When H. gets angry
he spits and fumes at my world, hates everyone he meets
who's alive, who's not yet under his spell.
Unabated, H. flies formless every morning from home to home
spreading poison: so easy in my world, ever so easy as he waits
for the gringos to destroy themselves, utterly. And then
the sun will come out for a while, and he'll leave.
From here, I am aware of God's crepuscular rays, the dark sun
    dance
creating for me heroes and signs in the day. So when the land's
    green
I know my demon will leave me for a while and I can speak again
as myself, never to be heard from, not a spirit. A suburban man
who reads the news: sometimes I wonder who won the Cold War!
I sit on spring days watching the rain, imagining
the soft roses I've discovered in this life.

To help you navigate these future waters you must know
of one sailor's journey. At last I was able to suffer the scattered
islands, and my demon sat on his oaken throne, red wings

folded, bones jutting widely from his dreadful face,
the foe of eternity grinning always at anything he knows
about suffering. Stories that are endless!
I, tale-turning Odysseus now, stood before the setting sun
outwitting everyone. Whole navies awaited me in the Caribbean
as I set sail on a whale, the dread Fedallah still lashed dead upon
    its brow.
At last I found the shore I most desire, and painfully,
while gathering fat crabs in the gravity-driven waves
found the sticks and remnants of my boat and crew.
Here I found Coyote cooking over a red fire she'd built
from the brig's main mast. As soon as the fire grew
she climbed over me quickly: in the sand we conceived
the next race to sail the coasts of Hell.

Disposal of the Poet's Body in the Desert

The afternoon I was burning
my mother placed me
into a tub of water and citrus fruit.

The effect was tremendous. So much
that when I die
rub me with oranges
to remind my body
of the sweet desert blooms
and the life I can't use.
O holy of holies
cleanse me next
with a warm wet cloth
wipe my tattoos clean
remind me of your hands
one more time.

To the West
I'll find a bed,
the remains of a rain pool
where my bones will grow old
like God's old tongue,
his whole fat face that I'll become.

Source Acknowledgments

The Americas Review, volume 25
Brujo Leaving Hawthorne's Woods, 1995
Letter from H. to the Faithful Who Await His Communiqués in Some
    Dim Future
  Reprinted with permission from the publisher of the *Americas Review*
    (Houston: Arte Público Press—University of Houston, 1999).

Blue Mesa Review, volume 7
Discovering a Christian Hymnal

Blue Mesa Review, volume 14
H. to His Children in the Year 2032

CALIBAN, volume 15
Cotton Train, Ramsey Co., Minnesota

Columbia, volume 30
Manifest of Boat Leaving on the Eve of the Third Millenium

Dislocate
Animal Time
On the Edge of Space, H. Speaks of the Infinite Void
To His Lords and Agents in the Field

Farrar, Straus and Giroux, LLC
Excerpt from "Dream Song #112," from *The Dream Songs,* by John
  Berryman. Copyright © 1969 by John Berryman. Copyright renewed
  1997 by Kate Donahue Berryman. Reprinted by permission.

Excerpt from *The Orange Tree,* by Carlos Fuentes, translated by Alfred
  Mac Adam. Translation copyright © 1994 by Farrar, Straus and
  Giroux, Inc. Reprinted by permission.

Luna, volume 5
La Chota Frega a Huitzilopochtli en el Camino
H. Is Bound and Stripped

Maverick Magazine, volume 1
Gift
A Letter to My Brothers and Sisters in North Korea

Maverick Magazine, volume 5
After Reading a Verse from the Holy Quran, Huitzilopochtli
   to His Scribes . . .

Midwest Quarterly, volume 36, no. 2
Downpour

South Dakota Review, volume 39, no. 3
H. Writes to Bear . . .
The Far Subdivisions

About the Author

Albino Carrillo was born in El Paso, Texas, in 1964 and grew up in Gallup and Albuquerque, New Mexico. He received a B.A. in English from the University of New Mexico in 1986 and a M.F.A. in Poetry from Arizona State University in 1993. From 1993 to 1995 he held a post-doctoral fellowship at Union College, New York, where he taught creative writing and American literature.

His poems have been published in numerous literary magazines, most recently *South Dakota Review, Blue Mesa Review,* the *Americas Review,* and *Columbia: A Journal of Art and Literature.* He has also published poems in the *Antioch Review, CALIBAN,* the *Midwest Quarterly, Sou'wester,* and *Puerto del Sol,* among others. His poems also have been anthologized in *Library Bound: A Saratoga Anthology,* part of the Hudson Valley Writers Series, published in cooperation with the Saratoga Springs Public Library. Along with the poet Jefferson Adams, he edits *Maverick Magazine: The Voice of American Poetic Arts.*

Carrillo is Assistant Professor in the Department of English at the University of Dayton in Ohio. Previously he taught in the English Department at the University of Minnesota. Currently he is writing *Antes de mi vida maldita,* a work of creative nonfiction set in the New Mexico and Arizona borderlands.